Just
in
Time

Video Resource

After the publication of his book, *Firstfruits Living,* the Churchwide Stewardship Council invited Lynn Miller to itinerate full-time as Firstfruits Teacher. Since 1992, Lynn has spoken to more than 250 congregations and conferences, with an estimated 20,000 participants, "to provoke unto love and to good works" (Heb. 10:24, KJV).

Because of his stimulating and dramatic style, many congregations requested that a videotape of these presentations be made available. Mennonite Board of Congregational Ministries has produced this video to enable other congregations and small groups to participate in this *Firstfruits Living* experience.

Firstfruits Living: The Video is distributed by Mennonite Media, 1251 Virginia Avenue, Harrisonburg, VA 22801. You may contact them for more information or to purchase this and other videos at 1-800-999-3534.

Price for the four videotapes in this series: $49.95 in U.S.; $71.95 in Canada.

Lynn A. Miller

Just
in
Time

Stories of God's Extravagance

Herald
Press

Scottdale, Pennsylvania
Waterloo, Ontario

Library of Congress Cataloging-in-Publication Data
Miller, Lynn A.
    Just in time : stories of God's extravagance / Lynn A. Miller.
       p. cm.
    ISBN 0-8361-9067-X (alk. paper)
    1. Stewardship, Christian. I. Title.
BV772.M519 1997
248'.6—dc21   97-954

The paper used in this publication is recycled and meets the minimum requirements of American National Standard for Information Sciences—Permanence of Paper for Printed Library Materials, ANSI Z39.48-1984.

Unless otherwise noted, Scripture quotations are from the *New American Standard Bible* (NASB), © The Lockman Foundation 1960, 1962, 1963, 1968, 1971, 1972, 1973, 1975, and are used by permission. NRSV, from the *New Revised Standard Version Bible,* copyright 1989 by the Division of Christian Education of the · National Council of the Churches of Christ in the USA, and used by permission.

JUST IN TIME
Copyright © 1997 by Herald Press, Scottdale, Pa. 15683
    Published simultaneously in Canada by Herald Press,
    Waterloo, Ont. N2L 6H7. All rights reserved
Library of Congress Catalog Number: 97-954
International Standard Book Number: 0-8361-9067-X
Printed in the United States of America
Book and cover design by Paula M. Johnson

06 05 04 03 02 01 00 99 98 97 10 9 8 7 6 5 4 3 2 1

To every person, disguised or not,
whose connection to
my travels
gave me these stories.

Contents

Preface

L ATE IN the spring of 1991, having survived a recent pastoral evaluation and comfortably settled into a new four-year contract, I went to my office on a Tuesday morning. The phone rang. It was God, pretending to be a fellow by the name of Ray Bair. (I know it was God because to this day Ray denies making that call!) In his best imitation of Ray's voice, God asked if I would consider taking on a full-time traveling job as a stewardship teacher for the Mennonite Church. Thus began nearly four years of traveling to over 200 churches and holding seminars and workshops about God's care for us.

At almost every assignment I learned something new about the topic. Sometimes there was a model of good stewardship already being lived out by one person or family. Sometimes I learned from the way a congregation worshiped or didn't. And sometimes insight came not from the congregation I was working with but just through something God arranged so I would learn something I needed to know for a future assignment.

Like the title story, "Just in Time." Not only did I learn the extent of God's care in those moments driving around Wausau, Wisconsin, with a man about to have a heart attack. I also learned about God's exquisite sense of timing. That crucial event took place right at the beginning of my assignment, when I needed to learn it most. The comforting sense of being in God's will and also in God's timing is what made possible my fulfilling the following years' commitments without falling apart from the stress of traveling and separation from those I loved most.

When the schedule occasionally made me despair (as during the six months in 1994 when I slept in my own bed only fifty nights), I remembered the words of Farah, the Muslim servant in the movie *Out of Africa:* "God is happy, M'sabu; he plays with us!" God is indeed happy. God delights in his children, and in his care for us we see his delight.

Disclaimers, Definitions, and Dedications

The first thing to say is that all these stories are true, especially the ones I made up. But the second thing to say is that I didn't make any up. Every story came from one of my assignments as an itinerant stewardship teacher from March 1992 to September 1995, and a few beyond. If you recognize yourself in one, and if your memory suggests that things might not have happened exactly the way I tell them, don't worry about it. It makes a better story this way!

A story, of course, is not just a narrative memory of an event. A story is a communicative form that has the power to change the lives of listeners. That is because we all live story-shaped lives, going from one event to another, surviving one tragedy after another, celebrating one victory after another.

However, when we ask the primal question Nicodemus put to Jesus, "How can this be?" we open ourselves to be changed by God's Spirit rather than just informed. Thus reflection is encouraged at the end of each narrative. Please take time to ponder those questions and listen for your own answers as to "how can these things be?"

The events from which these stories come would not have occurred without support of the following, to whom this book is dedicated and thanks are given:

The Churchwide Stewardship Council of the Mennonite Church, who invited me to leave a comfortable rural pastorate for a life on the road. Thank you for voicing God's call.

The 233 congregations that scheduled a Firstfruits seminar, then suffered the indignity of having me tell stories about them to the next congregation. Thank you for listening to the "hired gun" your leadership foisted on you.

The 150-plus families that opened their homes and their lives to me. Thank you for your outrageous hospitality (and I take back everything I said about your Hide-A-Bed).

Linda, my long-suffering wife, who endured my midweek two-day visits full of Thursday-evening complaints and Friday headaches. Thank you for making our home a place of refuge and rest. Surely there is a special reward for such great patience.

—*Lynn A. Miller*
  Chicago, Illinois

Just
in
Time

1

Just in Time

E ARLY IN 1992 I was the speaker at a regional conference near Glen Flora, Wisconsin. Because I had
two other assignments in Illinois the following week, I
drove, rather than flew, to northern Wisconsin. Near
Wassau late that evening I traveled through a heavy
thunderstorm, emerging on the other side into the
darkness of a cloudy sky.

Earlier that month the odometer on my old car had
turned over 200,000 miles. For the past several weeks
I'd had trouble with the alternator belt slipping. Then
the battery would run down if I drove with the lights
on. So I decided to stay the night in Wassau. I got off
the bypass at an exit surrounded by well-lit motel
signs. I pulled into the parking lot of an older motel ad-
vertising "clean rooms, $26.95," parked the car, and
walked to the office to register.

As I entered the office, the woman behind the
counter was dialing the telephone. Continuing to dial,

she pushed a blank registration card toward me and asked me to fill it out. As I began to write, she spoke urgently to someone, apparently the answering service of her family's physician.

"He's bleeding again," she said. "Can I speak to the doctor?" After a few seconds of listening, she said, "But I need to talk to him. He's bleeding quite a lot this time!"

Apparently the answering service gave her the number where her doctor could be reached. She said "Thank you" and put the receiver down.

She looked at me, said, "Would you please excuse me for a moment," and dialed again.

This time it was clear she had reached her physician. Once she described the problem her husband was having, she listened for a while, said "Thank you, I'll get him there as soon as I can," and hung up.

She picked up her phone book and began leafing through it. After a moment she looked up at me and said, "I'm sorry! My husband had laser surgery on his sinuses last January, and he has been bleeding from the incision on and off ever since. Now it's really bad. I need to find someone to get him to the emergency room." She started leafing through the phone book again.

After a few seconds of watching her look without success, I said, "How about me? I'll take him."

She raised her head and with a look of surprise said, "Would you?"

"Sure," I said, "Just hold a room for me. Where is he?"

When I made my offer, I thought he would be in a

back room of the office. But, to my dismay, she told me, "Get back on the freeway, go three exits south, take a left under the freeway, turn immediately right, and look for a house that you can't see for the bushes in front until you go past it." Seeing the distressed look on my face, she quickly drew the directions on the back of one of the motel's business cards.

So I got back into my old car with the slipping alternator belt, took the third exit south, turned left and went through the underpass, turned immediately right, went past the house because I couldn't see it for the bushes, turned around, found the driveway, and pulled up to the garage door. I arrived at the door just in time to meet a man coming out of the house with a bloody towel over his face and blood all over his shirt. I helped him into the car, then realized I didn't know where the hospital was.

He gave me directions in a muffled voice through the towel covering his face (which explains why I still don't have the faintest idea what he looks like). When we got to the hospital it was one giant construction zone, with hand-lettered signs pointing every which way to the emergency room entrance. When we finally found the ER door, a nurse was waiting with a wheelchair. She put him in it and told me to go park the car somewhere else, then come back to the waiting room.

When I got back, the receptionist sat down at her computer, looked at me, and said, "What's his name?"

"I don't know," I said.

"What's his address?"

"I don't know that either, but it's a house next to a Dairy Queen about three exits back down the freeway."

"Well, what's his wife's name?" she asked in a frustrated voice, apparently not finding enough room on the form to enter the kind of address I had given.

"I don't know," I said. Then, remembering the motel business card his wife had given me, I pulled it out of my pocket and gave it to her. I told her to call the number on the card as the man's wife was the night clerk there and couldn't leave her post. That, I explained, was why I, a stranger with nothing else to do, had brought the man in.

She took the card and told me I could leave.

When I got back to the motel, I went into the office. I told the woman that her husband was alright and at the emergency room. If she needed a ride home for him before midnight, she should call me and I'd get him. Otherwise, perhaps she could call a cab.

She thanked me and said, "I'd like to give you the room for free, but I'm just the night clerk, not the owner."

"I understand," I told her. I finished registering, took my key, and headed for my room.

The next morning, as I was loading my suitcase in the car, the woman came out of the office and walked across the parking lot toward me.

She said, "Good morning. I want to thank you for saving my husband's life last night."

"Well, it was just a nosebleed. No big deal."

"Oh no," she said. "Right after you left the hospital, he went into cardiac arrest. It was nip and tuck for awhile, but they say he's going to be okay. You got him there just in time."

Two strangers in an old car with a slipping alternator belt head down a dark freeway in northern Wisconsin. One is bleeding and about to have a heart attack. The other doesn't know where he is or where he is going. Yet just in time they find what they need.

That is what God's care for us is like. In his letter to the Romans, Paul speaks to the importance of the right timing in God's model of care. "For while we were still helpless, at the right time, Christ died for the ungodly" (5:6). Indeed, when we needed him most, he saved us. Thus God provides us with a model of his own stewardship, a model of timely, high-risk care.

2

Five Days (and Seven Potlucks) in Venice

A S NEAR AS I can tell, it all started during a meeting of denominational leaders in Oklahoma City. Someone had been describing a congregation's practice of members replacing vacations with work-service trips, some to spots as far away as eastern Europe. Then a woman from Mississippi said there was plenty of work to be done in her own area.

A pastor wondered, "Could you find me a place to send a team from my congregation?"

"How far are you willing to go?" she asked.

"How far do you have in mind?"

"Oh, only about as far as you can go in Louisiana. How about Venice, a little town at the end of the road that runs along the Mississippi? There's a small church there that needs help renovating an older building."

Off to Venice they went. One of this pastor's ideas was that the way to battle the cultural influences on his congregation's youth was to expand what "culture" meant. So the trip was scheduled for the week between Christmas and New Year's Day. Families as well as individuals were invited.

As it turned out, only four adults, one teenager, and a ten-year-old made up the team. But they were people who had given the first week of their yearly vacation time as an offering from their lives to God. This trip was a "firstfruit offering," an offering of that most basic commodity—time.

And did they have a time! After a twenty-hour drive south in a borrowed van through Kentucky, Tennessee, Mississippi, and Louisiana, they pulled into the parking lot of the Lighthouse Fellowship. For the next five days they received as well as gave. From the start they received the immediate, open friendship of their hosts. Working with them, they put a new gable front on the building, hung a new ceiling in the Sunday school wing, built several new storage closets, and installed a fold-up stairway that led into the attic.

Hosts and team devoured seven seafood potlucks in the five days they were there. They ate more kinds of seafood than most of the team knew existed. Four different kinds of shrimp, soft-shell crabs, oysters, several kinds of fish, and something delicious called "Alligator Sauce Picante" (since identified as "Road-kill Gumbo").

They heard stories of the kind that should be true if they aren't! The pastor was a professional shrimp fisherman, and he and his congregation kept the visitors enthralled with one Cajun story after another. If you missed Barbara telling what happened when "Plue" kept yelling "Turn the wheel, turn the wheel" while they were shrimping, you missed something special.

Maybe that is what God meant when he had Paul write to the Corinthian church to tell them that the one who "sows bountifully will reap bountifully" (2 Cor. 9:6). When the members of the team sowed bountifully by giving up the first week of their yearly vacations to help someone else, they reaped bounty beyond compare in the new friendships they now have and will keep into eternity.

3

Learning the Language

S OMETIMES TRAVELING across the country with the message of firstfruits living seems a lot like travelling through the different countries of Europe or Africa. As soon as you cross another border, you have to start speaking a new language. As any seasoned traveler can tell you, if you want to be understood, you need to "learn the language."

Early in September I crossed a border in my travels and promptly found I should have taken the time to learn the language. One early fall evening I spoke at a combined dinner meeting of Sarasota area pastors, church leaders, and members of the local chapter of MEDA (Mennonite Economic Development Associates). This was not the first time I had appeared before a MEDA group, but it was the first time I had spoken to them about stewardship issues. Right in the middle of the event, I discovered that I should have learned the language first.

My assignment was to examine God's model of stewardship as seen in his sacrifice of Jesus on the cross. God, I suggested, was operating as an "entrepreneur" rather than a "conservative investor." Jesus (God's entire supply of venture capital) was put at risk on the cross for us despite our being "sinners and enemies of God" at the time. So God took a great risk for the possibility of great return.

I developed the point that God's persistent grace comes from God's character rather than from the profit motive or success of the venture. Since millions and billions of people have gone to their graves without Jesus Christ, in business terms God has "failed." By the looks on their faces, I immediately knew that when I said *failed*, I was speaking the wrong language.

I was trying to say that despite God's foreknowledge that billions of people would seek salvation elsewhere (in false religions, materialism, atheism), God offered up his Son anyway. Maybe I should have said, "Despite the most accurate market research in the world, research that clearly showed a poor market share of the potential customer base, the manufacturer went into production anyway." The embarrassing fact is that if salvation was a hamburger, most of the world's population in the past two thousand years has been buying their hamburgers elsewhere.

However, we are the ones to be embarrassed, not God. For in this case, it is the sales force (evangelists) of the company (kingdom) who have failed. The manufacturer (God) made an extremely effective product (the atonement), and expected, even commanded, that it be distributed primarily by the referrals (testimonies) of satisfied customers (the saved). So what is the problem?

Perhaps it's because we have focused on the terminal benefit (heaven) rather than the product's living reality (Christ's lordship). Perhaps if we begin demonstrating (making manifest) that the immediate product benefit (Jesus as Lord) has set us free to give away our lives (in stewardship), we will find demand catching up with supply!

4

The Two Tomatoes: A Story So Good It Must Have Happened

A T LEAST ONCE a week for several years, I told my audiences a story about two tomatoes. I told the story so often because it is the most effective way I know of emotionally portraying the difference between a firstfruit gift and any other.

The story of "The Two Tomatoes" was written by Ray and Lillian Bair of Elkhart, Indiana, as a play with two short acts. The first act takes place late in the summer. Someone offers a neighbor a tomato from the "buckets and buckets" he has left over.

The second act takes place early the next summer. The same person offers the same neighbor the first ripe tomato from his garden. At that point in the story,

I can usually actually see the difference between the two tomatoes in the faces of the audience.

This little play illustrates well both the specialness of things that are first and the feeling of specialness that comes from receiving a firstfruits gift. It is truly one of those stories that is so good that if it didn't happen, it should have!

Then, right in the middle of one August in Indiana, it did! Before I had the chance to tell the tomato story to a Fort Wayne congregation, the pastor got up during sharing time and told this story.

"Last week," he said, "our family got a phone call from a member of the congregation. She was checking to see if we were home because she wanted to bring us a gift. But when she came, all she had in her hand was one small, barely ripe tomato. She explained that she knew it wasn't much of a gift. It was a smallish tomato and only one at that. But she told us it was a very special tomato. For this tomato was the very first tomato to ripen in her whole garden."

Then, with obvious emotion, that pastor talked about how special that special gift had made him and his family feel. He looked at me and said he hoped he hadn't ruined anything I was about to say in the sermon, but that somehow he thought he now knew what a firstfruit was.

During the week before a speaking assignment, I am aware of God preparing me for my task. In Fort Wayne in the middle of August, I was also made very much aware that God had been busy preparing the congregation as well. Another example of the exhaustive care exhibited by an extravagant God.

5

Something to Do the Rest of Your Life

I KNEW IT WAS going to happen sooner or later. After all, considering that I had at that point preached the firstfruits message in seventy congregations to over eleven thousand people, it was bound to happen. I thought I was prepared for it. But when it actually happened, it scared me nonetheless.

It happened in Minnesota, of all places. Midway through my time with a congregation, I had proposed that retirement was the "abundance" of one's life (2 Cor. 9:8) and that the purpose for that abundance was to give it away in our lifestyle of "good works" (Eph. 2:10). The "inheritances" were designed to help one's children get a good start on their adult life, rather than a bonus in the beginning of their retirement years. That was when it happened! Someone took what I said seriously enough to *do* something about it!

I found myself sitting in a living room trying to help a newly retired couple decide exactly what to do with their abundance of both years and money. They agreed they had already given their children their inheritances by ensuring they all had the resources to be educated and off on their own. They also agreed that although they had recently moved from the farm to town, they were not ready to begin looking for a soft place to lie down before they fell down (my description of what retirement has come to mean for far too many of us). But they didn't exactly know how to make the alternative happen.

It was at the end of that afternoon that I got scared. These two believers decided to donate their farmland to a charitable foundation. They would put the little checkbook of "Recommendations for Disbursement" that came with their gift in their suitcase, then hit the road looking for good works to get involved in and spend their abundance on. Because they intend to go out the way they came in, with a zero balance, the only thing they are worried about is that they might not have enough time to get the job done. So they have told the foundation what to do with whatever is left when they are gone.

I guess I should have been better prepared for the shock of having someone actually do something about what they had heard. And I should have expected that sooner or later someone would. What a way to spend the rest of your life!

6

A Ready Market

ONE OF the more mysterious discoveries made during my original study of the theme of first-fruits was found in the book of Acts. My discovery was that the first preaching of the apostles of Jesus Christ was focused on the resurrection of Christ rather than the cross on which he was crucified. In fact, Peter announces in Acts 1:21-22 that the job description of the new apostle chosen to replace Judas is to be "a witness with us of His resurrection."

Acts 2:23-24 notes that he was crucified and killed "by the hands of godless men." But the focus is that "God raised Him up again, putting an end to the agony of death." When introducing a quotation from King David in verse 31, Peter says that David "spoke of the resurrection of the Christ." And in verse 32, Peter refers once more to the resurrection without reference to the cross: "This Jesus God raised up again, to which we are all witnesses."

In one reference after another throughout Acts, the apostles witness to the resurrection of Christ, then eventually to the future resurrection of the dead as well as Christ. Most strikingly, in 5:30-31 the apostles refer to the resurrection of Christ and his exaltation at God's right hand "to grant repentance to Israel, and forgiveness of sins." This ties the resurrection to forgiveness of sin, something the following two thousand years of theological development reserved for his death on the cross.

So were the apostles wrong? Hadn't they had time to think clearly about what happened at the cross? Or were they onto something we have missed in our subsequent mental gymnastics?

At a firstfruits seminar in Chesapeake, Virginia, a question from the congregation about this mystery sparked a discussion that gave us all new appreciation for the wisdom of the apostles. "Could it have been that the resurrection was the thing foremost on their minds?"

That started us thinking about what it is that makes something "foremost" on one's mind. Our exciting conclusion was this: You have to convince people there is a future price they will pay for sin before you can expect them to want the forgiveness bought by Christ's sacrifice on the cross. But you don't have to convince anyone that they will physically die. Everyone knows they are going to die; the evidence is all around us. Therefore, there is a ready market for the good news of the resurrection, first Christ's resurrection, then our own!

Of course, once you realize that the "hope of the

resurrection" involves the resurrection of both the righteous and the wicked, then you are in the market for whatever it is that moves you from "wickedness" to "righteousness."

So the apostles were pretty smart after all. The good news of Christ the firstfruits of the dead is the logical first step to proclaiming the second step, that "Jesus died for your sins." You know, if I keep this up long enough and listen to enough congregations, I might learn something about firstfruits after all!

7

"Doing Well" Versus "Doing Good"

E VERY ONCE in a while someone, usually a person in business, reminds me that "Time is money." For a long time I accepted that. But a businessman said something that made me rethink this.

In spring 1993 my wife and I made plans to spend December and January working on a short-term service project in southern Asia. I had this crazy idea about building small fishing boats out of water hyacinth fibers and fiberglass resin. And we had an invitation to visit friends living and working in Calcutta, India.

I described our plans for those two months to my successful friend, whose disposable income is at least three or four times mine. He looked at me with jealousy and said, "I wish I were as rich as you must be."

That was when I began to understand the relationship between time and money in a different way. It seems the sages are at least half right. Time is indeed money. By spending time working, you gain money. But sadly, it doesn't seem to work well the other way around. Time may be money, but money isn't time. You might get money by spending time working, but you can't buy much time by spending money.

Time comes from God, and stewardship is the process we engage in as we make choices as to how we spend what God has given us. My friend willingly spends most of his time making a great deal of money, which he then shares generously. But he is also envious of the time I have to spend in a service project.

When I suggested that in the future he might want to spend less time making money and more time doing something else, he corrected me by stating the obvious. Most businesses, he said, must be operated year-round just to stay afloat.

This says to me that Christians, created by God "in Christ Jesus for good works, which God prepared beforehand to be our way of life" (Eph. 2:10), should be careful to choose occupations that allow us to spend time "doing good" as well as "doing well."

Yes, time is money, but you can't have all you want of both. Choosing when "enough is enough" of either might be one of the more crucial decisions we make. Arranging our lives so God's time can be spent in God's plan seems to be the doorway to being in God's will.

8

Roast Lamb and Fresh Bread

E VERY ONCE in awhile, right in the middle of a worship service, I have the strangest feeling that it probably was a lot more fun worshiping in the tabernacle in the desert. Just think of all the neat stuff they did back then during worship services. People brought all kinds of things to give to God, and they gave it in all kinds of ways.

For example, when the tabernacle was established, two lambs a day were offered to the Lord, one in the morning and one in the evening. The morning lamb was to be offered with a measure of choice flour mixed with oil and wine. The evening lamb was to be offered with grain and drink.

The grain offering itself must have smelled wonderful, mixed with frankincense, then baked in an oven. The first of the ears of grain were brought as a firstfruits offering, and incense was burnt on a special altar. To complete the offering, money was given to God as well, half a shekel per person, no more, no less.

The priests, not to speak of God to whom all this was given, must have reveled in the mouth-watering aroma of roast lamb, sweet corn, freshly baked perfumed breads—all accompanied by the tinkling sound of silver coins and the sweet smell of burning incense. What an amazing collection of delights for the senses.

Now I suppose that the reason I sometimes think of all this right in the middle of a worship service is that frankly most offerings today seem bland compared to those earlier ones. What do we usually do? The ushers come forward, someone mumbles something about the budget and the deficit or the poor and the hungry. Someone else plays some funeral prelude music. This is so we will all have our heads in our laps and not see what our neighbor is putting in the plate, which promptly disappears out the back of the sanctuary so the treasurer can count it during the sermon and get to Sunday dinner on time with the rest of us.

Next week, at the bottom of the second page of the bulletin, there will be a little notice: last week's offering totaled so many dollars and so many cents. As my daughters used to say, "Boooooorrrrring!"

I don't know who said an offering has to be boring. In fact, the more I listen, the more voices I hear indicating that some of us would like to do it differently. For example, in Milford, Nebraska, three farmers came to me after an evening meeting and asked why they couldn't put the scale ticket from the first truckload of corn harvested that fall into the offering plate. The corn wouldn't be sold until next spring when the prices are better, but they wanted to give the grain itself to the Lord immediately. Their goals were both to celebrate the harvest and to return to God the first of it.

In Blooming Glen, Pennsylvania, a young man asked why he couldn't write down his offering of the one day a month he was going to give the church by working with the custodian. Another young man, a dairy farmer, came up with the idea of putting in the offering plate the receipt for the first tank of milk each year. And in Ohio a woman asked me why the Women's Sewing Circle couldn't put the quilt they had worked so hard on and were now donating to a fund-raising auction into the offering plate as well.

Why not, indeed? If the offering is given to God rather than the budget or the treasurer, then anything we want to give to God can and should be part of it.

The only thing we pastors will have to do is make sure we have big enough offering plates and strong enough ushers to receive it all. Then we need to do the most important thing of all—get out of the way and let God be glorified!

Oh, I almost forgot. There is one more thing. We will also need a lot more space at the bottom of the second page of the bulletin. Because next week we will have to report—

LAST WEEK'S OFFERING

> 3,000 bushels of firstfruits corn,
> Thirteen hours of voluntary service,
> Two quilts,
> Six bushels of apples,
> Four hundred gallons of milk, and
> A whole bunch of money.

Come to think of it, that might even make up for the missing smell of roast lamb and freshly baked bread.

9

Finding Community
on the Road

TAKING ON an itinerant ministry is a lot like buying a "pig in a poke." You really don't know what you have until you open the bag and hit the road. I knew I was going to be gone from home a lot and doing a lot of driving. I knew I was going to be meeting a lot of new people. But I didn't know how much I would miss being part of my own worshiping community.

I have long understood that a core definition of Anabaptism is that the church is found where the community of God gathers to worship. What I didn't realize was how important being a part of a consistent worshiping community would become to me. After the first six months of being the Stewardship Council's firstfruits teacher, I discovered that the unpleasant empty feeling growing inside of me was there because

I no longer belonged anywhere. I was a man without a community.

And so, in the middle of October, between assignments in northern Indiana, I arranged to spend three days at the Hermitage near Three Rivers, Michigan. I hoped to find something to heal that growing woundedness inside.

After a day of walking and getting quiet inside, then two hours with Mary Herr, one of the two resident spiritual directors, I began to read. Mary had pointed me to the writings of Esther de Waal, an Englishwoman who used the Rule of St. Benedict to help herself find stability in her busy vocation as teacher, author, mother, and wife. At one point in her book, de Waal referred to Catherine Doherty's writings about the Russian tradition of the "Poustinia."

While reading the book *Poustinia*, I discovered the word literally means "desert" and refers to the hut in the woods near a village to which a person would retreat and spend time with God. But this Russian hermitage differed from the Middle Eastern hermitage in that the Poustiniki was not isolated from village life. Rather, he or she was always available to assist whoever asked for help. The Poustiniki were expected to give whatever help was needed, whether getting the hay in before a rain or spiritual guidance in times of emotional distress. Most crucial of all, the Poustiniki's main task was to "make Christ more present."

After digesting this idea of the "Poustinia in the marketplace" overnight, on the third day of my stay, I began to walk with my thoughts, one in particular. Doherty speaks of the vocation of the "apostolate" (those who are sent out) and refers to Paul's claim that he is "working to make up what is lacking in Christ's afflictions." Curious about what possibly could be "lacking" in the suffering of our Lord, I turned to Colossians 1:24-27 and read as I walked.

> I am now rejoicing in my sufferings for your sake, and in my flesh I am completing what is lacking in Christ's afflictions for the sake of his body, that is, the church. Of this church I was made a minister according to the stewardship from God bestowed on me for your benefit, that I might fully carry out the preaching of the word of God, the mystery that has been hidden from the past ages and generations, but has now been revealed to his saints. To them God willed to make known what is the riches of the glory of this mystery among the Gentiles, which is Christ in you, the hope of glory. (NRSV/NASB)

While I was reading and walking down Dutch Settlement Road, God began to speak to me. As ministers called by God's stewardship, "Christ in us" is our community on the road. Though we are absent from our regular worshiping community, we are present with the One we consistently worship in our traveling Poustinia. Although we are apart from the gathered assembly of the believers we know, we are together with the One we believe in.

So I now rejoice anew that I do this work, in some way completing what Christ began at the cross. For I have been called to this ministry through the very stewardship of God. I am sustained by a new sense of "God with me." I know I carry within me a "Hermitage of the Heart," the mystery of Christ in me.

10

A Travel Agent in Every Congregation

ONE OF the most striking quotes I have ever heard at a graduation ceremony was, "I stand on the brink of a great career. Won't someone please push me in!" And one of the most exciting parts of what I get to do as a minister is to look for people standing on the brink who just need a little push.

In eastern Pennsylvania a young man asked if I would have breakfast with him. He wanted to "pick my brain," to explore something I had said during the Sunday morning message. So we met at 8:00 a.m. that Tuesday morning. Following our meeting, I had the distinct impression that if I hadn't pushed him over the brink, I at least shoved him closer to the edge.

The idea in my message that interested him was that each congregation could send out groups of people to service opportunities or mission experiences. He was interested because in the coming year he was planning to go to Nepal for a visit with a missionary and to Brownsville, Texas, to work on a Habitat for Humanity house. Although he wasn't aware of it, all during our conversation I could see the beginnings of one of those groups at his congregation.

My experience has been that the most difficult obstacle to sending out people is finding someone with time and talent to organize the trip. Most pastors are already overextended and most adult members overbusy. So asking pastors or volunteers to take on a new task is often a fruitless and frustrating task.

But in most congregations there are people who are already organizing and taking their own trips for a variety of reasons. Many of these people are seasoned travelers, already good at making travel arrangements and getting around in new situations. Some already have a personal interest in extending the realm of God throughout the world.

These are the natural organizers of sending groups. The young man with whom I was having breakfast was one of these people. All he needed was a small shove into the role of inviting others to go with him on his trips. I suggested that his next step might be to develop a printed catalog of next year's trips that each family could have in front of them as they planned their coming vacations.

That's all it takes. Just one person already doing something. A willingness to invite others to come along. And of course someone to push them over the edge into being their congregation's "travel agent."

_11_

The First One Through

O NE OF the ways I have kept myself sane over the last ten years is by building and sailing small wooden boats. I usually limit myself to sailing in inland lakes and occasionally in lakes Erie and Michigan. But somewhere in the Gulf of Mexico there is an island I am going to sail to someday. For I am told that on this island there is an underwater cave more beautiful than any dryland cave so far discovered.

They tell me that you can sail into the shallow water of a well-protected cove and anchor near a cliff wall. Then you dive off your boat, swim to the face of the cliff, take several deep breaths, dive down, and swim into an opening in the rock wall. After ten or fifteen seconds of hard underwater swimming, you surface inside the most beautiful space this side of heaven. Those who have been there speak endlessly of the glorious sights beheld in that underwater cave.

But how was that cave discovered? Who was the

first one to make that underwater journey? How did that first person through the cave know there was an airspace inside? The first person into the cave must have had a lot of faith that what was in there was worth the risk of finding it. And everyone since owes that person a debt for showing the rest of us that it is possible to reach the wonders that await us.

One part of God's care for us is like that. In some ways, death is a tunnel that leads to a place none of us have been to before. We really don't know how long the tunnel is or what is at the end of it. Blessedly, however, someone has been through to the other end. That someone came back out, stands at the entrance, and says, "Don't worry, it's only a short swim." Jesus, the resurrected Christ, has already been there. He can tell us that all we need to do is "have faith, pray, hold your breath, and you'll come through to the other end in fine shape."

In raising Jesus from the dead, God stewarded us through our own fear of death. Jesus is God's firstfruits offering, the evidence that we have nothing to fear from death. "As a matter of fact, Christ has been raised from the dead, the firstfruits of those who have died" (1 Cor. 15:20).

12

Prudence and the Gardens

T HE FIRST SESSION of most of the firstfruits seminars I do serves as the Sunday morning sermon.
Since there will be more people in that session than
any other, I try to make sure everyone has a clear intro-
duction to firstfruits stewardship. But I also want those
who do not attend the following sessions to take away
something practical. So I have developed a small
"sticky-back" handout entitled, "How to Spend Your
Life." It's designed to remind us of the three divisions
in God's "economy" outlined in 2 Corinthians 9:8—
worship, needs, and abundance for good works.

But occasionally an older person will challenge my
proposition that in God's economy there will be God's
money to give away for God's good works. "What
about prudence?" They challenge me to consider ex-

pensive nursing-home care, and that through insurance we can share that expense. I answer that only a
minority of us need such care.

When they state that they do not want to burden
their children, I reply that "I lay awake nights thinking
of ways to be a burden to my children." That does not
seem to work either. Prudence carries more weight
than statistics or humor.

A friend, Weldon Schlonenger, pastor of a rural Illinois Mennonite congregation and practical theolo-
gian, mentions another possibility for addressing
anxieties about the future. Prudence, he says, is a virtue. But, he continues, "all vice is exaggerated virtue."

Weldon points us to the example of the serpent in
the garden of Eden. He says, "The woman and then the
man did not eat the forbidden fruit because they were
reckless, illogical risk-takers. They ate because they
wanted the control and safety and security that come
with knowledge. They wanted the power to control
their own destinies. Consider the possibility that the
essence of original sin is an overdose of prudence!"

Aha! Prudence, financial planning, even the dread-
ed profit-motive are not in themselves evil. But when
used to grasp control over the future that belongs to
God, they become sin itself. And so we are transported
from one garden (Eden) to another (Gethsemane).
From "in the day that you eat from it your eyes will be
opened, and you will become like God, knowing good
and evil." *To* "if Thou art willing, remove this cup from
Me; yet not My will, but Thine be done."

Prudence has its place. But not as a substitute for
faith. Where faith will lead us, prudence cannot go.

13

Jesus Is the Key

SITTING ON the keyboard of my badly outdated (but completely sufficient) Apple II+ computer is a brand new skeleton key. I know it's new because I know when it was made and who made it. In the middle of one recent October, I was speaking at a congregation south of Lancaster, Pennsylvania. On Thursday I was invited to the home of Weaver and Helen Reitz for the evening meal.

After we had eaten, Weaver invited me into his basement. There he showed me his hobby of casting small items in pewter. And one of the many pewter items he gave me that Thursday evening was a shiny new skeleton key.

The key quickly became one of the most treasured possessions I regularly carry in my travels. Not because any particular lock is opened by the key, but because on the side of the key in raised letters it says, "JESUS IS THE KEY."

That is an important thing for us who teach in the area of stewardship to remember. *Jesus is the key*! It's important because of all people we are tempted to go to the wisdom of almost anyone other than Jesus for advice on stewardship matters. You only have to look at the Scripture index of most money-management books to see that the missing authority is the One whose name we bear, Jesus the Christ. That is doubly tragic, because Jesus has a lot to say about financial stewardship.

For example, in Matthew 26:6-13 the story is told of the woman who came to Jesus in the home of Simon the leper with "an alabaster vial of very costly perfume." After she poured it on his head, the disciples became indignant. "Why this waste?" they cried. Jesus' reply that "she has done a good deed to Me" challenges our beliefs that occasional extravagance is waste and frugality is faithfulness.

Jesus is telling us that the real value of something is not in its content but in our intent. When we read that story, we find that the primary beneficiary of godly stewardship has shifted from us to him, from *doing well* to *doing good*. That is the key to Christian stewardship: it is defined by the word of Christ rather than the wisdom of Solomon, David, or anyone else.

So I intend to keep in my pocket that shiny new skeleton key Weaver made. Mainly, I want it to remind me that Jesus is the Key. But I also want the key to unlock me from my preoccupation with the technical contents of stewardship. Then I will be set free to be extravagant in doing the work of Jesus.

14

No Free Lunch

ONE OF the lessons I have learned is about the ability of congregational members to give more of either their time or money in response to an increased budget, an emotional appeal, or even one of my seminars. Almost everyone has almost all of their time and money already allocated somewhere else.

For example, even when we just sit motionless in front of the TV, we are using all the time we have. Likewise, all our money goes somewhere. I have yet to find people who have piles of cash lying around, waiting to be used. "Free" time and "extra" income are like a vacuum. Their very existence attracts activity and expenditure. Something rushes in to fill the void.

A case in point. Because of the cancellation of one of my commitments, I had an extra four weeks of unassigned time right in the middle of a recent summer. Four weeks not committed to any project or pressing commitment. There was nothing on "standby." It was too late to arrange anything. Four weeks to relax. Time perhaps to sit back and reflect on the past several years. Some quality "free time" at last!

But on the first day of the first uncommitted week, a friend who happens to be a farmer told me in a casual conversation that he was planning to burn down a large wooden corncrib to build a new garage. After looking at the crib, I asked my friend if I might take it down before he burned it, to use the material for a boat-building shed. He agreed. In the next four weeks, I tore it down, took the lumber home, and put it back up as a barn. At the end of the summer I had a new barn, but not much relaxation or reflection.

All the time or money God has given us will be used somehow. This means a life of stewardship is a matter of making choices about where we spend our time and money—and where we don't! To do one thing, we must choose not to do something else. To give more here, we must spend less there.

Somehow that seems to be as it should be. After all, Jesus said that to save our lives we would need to lose them first (Matt. 16:25). Sort of an early version of "there's no such thing as a free lunch." Everything costs something. Being stewards means making choices that will cost us something somewhere.

That is why true generosity, generosity in the model of the cross, is valuable. It costs something. And so, although there might not be any such thing as a "free" lunch, that just makes the "lunch" even more valuable.

15

Only If You Don't Enjoy It

O NE OF the books of the Bible that I quote from a lot is 2 Chemicals. In 2 Chemicals are all the verses about stewardship that we hold so dear and believe so fervently, verses found nowhere else in the Bible. Second Chemicals 3:16 says, "It's good stewardship if you got it on sale." Likewise, 2 Chemicals 4:21 advises, "Frugality is next to cleanliness, which is next to godliness."

However, recently I discovered a new 2 Chemicals verse which goes, "It's okay to be extravagant with yourself only if you don't enjoy it and if it serves someone else."

This verse was quoted during our final meal at a hotel where a stewardship conference was being held. The Sunday seafood buffet was the obvious pride and joy of the hotel kitchen. What a buffet it was! Snow crab legs. Raw, steamed, and fried oysters. Three or four kinds of shrimp. Lobster tail, fresh fish, and several dishes I had never heard of before.

Now this extravaganza was not a $3.95 special. It was priced at $14.95. Considering the supply of seafood in the middle of Oklahoma, it was probably worth every penny. I did consider partaking, but I also considered that I would be spending the next three or four hours sitting in an airplane. To preserve my intestinal comfort, I ordered the fruit plate.

But the sight of my fruit plate was a source of no small internal conflict for some people. A number of those who had decided to have the seafood buffet felt it necessary to explain to me that although they were having that most sumptuous seafood feast, they really weren't enjoying it. They had made that choice because, as one person put it, "The kitchen had gone to so much trouble." Somehow that made it okay!

Isn't that interesting! To justify indulging ourselves in a moment of occasional extravagance, we feel we need to convince others (and maybe ourselves) that we really aren't enjoying ourselves but are serving others. Why? Is it our years of learning those 2 Chemicals verses at our mothers' knees? Are we now firmly convinced that God gives special favor to those who "do without"? Or is it strong guilt over simple enjoyment?

Whatever the reasons, I wish we could get over it! I see nothing ungodly or evil in occasional extravagance. Isn't the cross a moment of God's extravagance on our behalf? Jesus is not on sale at the cross. God is not offering us a $3.95 special in the death of his Son. The last thing God wants us to feel in our salvation experience is guilt, as if it's okay to be saved only if we don't enjoy it. Paul prays that the "God of hope will fill us with all joy and peace in [our] believing" (Rom. 15:13).

But a word of warning is in order. Continual extravagance is simply high living. Then the specialness quickly fades. So the word *occasional* is important. It means "carefully choosing" is as important as "thoroughly enjoying." This makes occasional extravagance a moment of godly stewardship.

16

Firstfruits of the Gospel, Indian Style

I T'S AMAZING how often the little things you get involved in turn into the more significant moments of your life. Such was the case during a winter 1993-1994 visit to India. My assignment was to evaluate replacement housing relief efforts following such natural disasters as flood or fire. But it was one of those "Oh, by the way" things that really made the trip worthwhile.

When I arrived in Calcutta, we discussed what I would do. At the end of the conversation, the visit coordinator said, "By the way, you will also be giving seven hours of input at the Mennonite Church of India's Peace Conference in Dhamtari."

After recovering from surprise, I planned those seven hours. I decided to spend five sessions on firstfruits stewardship and the last two hours asking them to define for themselves the firstfruits of the gospel for India. What is the core of biblical truth for the whole world? How is it best said in post-missionary India?

That is what we did in Dhamtari. I gave my normal seminar presentation, then directed their efforts at coming up with an "Indian Statement of Faith." After a great deal of discussion and some helpful historical and cultural background from a founding bishop, the following statement was agreed upon.

"We believe that the Bible teaches that Jesus is God's Messiah, who came to suffer and die for the forgiveness of sins, and who calls us to be missionaries of God's love and service."

Beyond the obvious cross-cultural character of this statement, there is also a significant contextual stewardship of the gospel going on here. Indian culture is broad and diverse, with strong Hindu and Muslim influences. But in that multicultural mix there exists a common appreciation for a number of "spiritual" values. These include the importance of holy writings, the suffering of a messiah figure for others, and a life of service in a response to God's love.

What does that have to do with stewardship? Well, to be a steward means to care for and manage what God has given to us. In restating the truths of God's love in their own context, these Indian pastors have moved beyond the foundational phase of the missionary movement in India. They are themselves becoming stewards of their own good news from God. When they proclaim the gospel of Jesus Christ in those words, they offer the firstfruits of their own labor. They literally become stewards of the gospel.

17

The Business of Generosity

❖

O NE OF the big surprises for those who have done
well financially is that giving away money is almost as much work as making it. I have met more than
one businessperson who has become cynical trying to
do good with the proceeds of having done well. On my
assignments I often meet separately with businesspeople of the church to help them deal with the business
of generosity.

They feel worn-out in doing good. Much of this
comes from having to deal with the work giving away
money involves. Most businesspeople find that it takes
almost as much management skill and time to be a
good steward as it did to produce the profit. Much of
the cynicism comes from the barrage of requests from
well-meaning fund-raisers representing thousands

__ _n thousands of ministries and institutions needing God's abundance for their work.

But a growing number of "benefactors" have discovered that a little planning can make the business of benevolence become a blessing. One of them, Maynard Sauder, CEO of Sauder Manufacturing in Archbold, Ohio, told me that being generous with a company's profits can be a lot of fun as well as profitable for the kingdom—if the several things are kept in mind.

First, you need to have a process for receiving and considering requests. Nothing is more stressful than having to decide on the phone or in the fund-raiser's presence how to respond. Share the load of deciding. Set regular meeting times for those decisions so you can honestly respond, "I appreciate knowing about your needs. We'll be glad to consider a written request from you at the next meeting."

Second, have a focus in mind. Decide what you will be concentrating on in your generosity. It could be as broad as missions or as narrow as dental services in rural Honduras. This will allow you not only to fulfill some personal interests but also to respond to some requests by saying, "Thank you for your request, but our current focus is elsewhere." Keep in mind that you aren't the only company being asked to help. Therefore a project's success doesn't depend only on you.

Third, get personally involved in the project, or at least make a follow-up visit to see how your generosity is being used. At Sauder Manufacturing a group of employees make a yearly request for funds to build medical clinics in the Dominican Republic. When they return, they give a report to the entire company. This gives the corporation both personal involvement and a system of accountability.

Finally, don't make a law of the above. Be flexible so you can occasionally respond to an immediate, personal appeal, even to something outside your generosity focus. And don't be afraid to make an offer of assistance different from the first request. Be creative. Offer more, less, or an alternate approach.

The business of being generous is supposed to be fun. "God loves a cheerful giver." My experience shows that cheerfulness comes more from one's attitude and a little planning, than from the amount of the check.

18

Adding Community to Generosity (and How to Get the IRS to Chip In)

W HEN I COME to a congregation to help them struggle with the question of how we can all become better stewards in God's kingdom, I spend the first three hours making sure we have correctly answered the "why" question. "Why be good stewards in the first place?"

If stewardship is a life of responding in thankfulness to what God has already done in our lives, we need to remind ourselves exactly what God *has* done. Then we can turn to the more technical aspect of the "how" question.

For most of us, the "how" of our charitable activity consists of individually making simple cash contributions to persons or institutions. But I have recently discovered that cheerfulness in giving is multiplied when we join others in passing on Christ's generosity.

We have long known that giving things rather than cash can multiply both the fun and amount of our charity. Farmers who give commodities to a charitable gift fund avoid federal, state, local, and self-employment taxes on the sale of those commodities (greatly increasing the gift since those taxes can often approach 50 percent). They can also recommend where they want the proceeds from selling those commodities to go.

Persons with stock certificates, land, or anything that has increased in value since its purchase can likewise increase their contribution by giving them instead of cash. This is because they both avoid the capital gains taxes and can take a cash contribution deduction on their federal income taxes. (Note: These examples were current in 1995. Check for changes made in the law since then before applying them to your situation.)

At least some of the added pleasure I get from using these techniques comes from knowing that by using the tax law to do good, I can offset the more questionable things my tax dollars end up supporting.

But the real multiplication of joy in generosity for me came when a group of young farm families at a congregation near Lancaster, Pennsylvania, came up with the idea of forming a "generosity" club. These families combine their gifts of milk and eggs and stock shares and whatever into one account. Then they meet quarterly over a Sunday dinner to decide how to give away what they have donated. Since a foundation's cost in administering a charitable gift fund is the same no matter how large the account, these families have reduced those costs to a fourth of what they would be if each had their own account.

What a kick! Not only are they getting the IRS to contribute to their generosity, they are also helping their denomination's foundation keep the costs of being charitable as low as possible. If giving away more money at less cost isn't a principle of good stewardship found in Scripture somewhere, it ought to be!

19

The Mixed Blessing of Being Taken Seriously

F OR THE PAST several years I have ended almost every firstfruits seminar with a session entitled "How to Give Your Life Away." During this hour I lead the congregation through practical ways of giving their lives away. I describe how others have made gifts of their time and money. I describe one congregation's "Firstfruits Saturday Bunch"—men who set aside the first Saturday of each month to work on someone else's house.

I describe what "Vacations with a Purpose" look like. You reap generously when you sow generously by using your vacation time to work with people who need your help, rather than going to Orlando to be entertained by people who just want your money. I always encourage people to visit the missionaries they and their congregation support, if they can do so.

Then near the end of that last session, I offer what I think is a more biblical way to see the progression of one's life. This way is based on responding to God's calls throughout life rather than seeing life as made up of work and retirement. To describe the latter, I draw on the chalkboard the following time line of the typical North American life.

Birth	20-25	Work	50-55	Work	65	Retirement	Death
	you leave home		your children leave home			your parents die, you receive your inheritance	

Then I draw another diagram, making sure people see the differences in when you receive your inheritance (when you leave home and need it, rather than when your parents die). More importantly, I show what a more biblical goal might be. This is to follow God's call rather than accumulating more material security. I speak of the first call, which involves the heart of your working years, and the second call, which takes place after you have fulfilled the first.

Birth	20-25	First Call	50-55	Second Call	Death
	you leave home, receive inheritance		children leave home, receive inheritance		

I then spend a few moments describing how you decide when you have accomplished your First Call. That is when you have—

1. Given your children their "inheritance" (what they need to live adult, self-supporting lives, such as an education, help in starting a business, farming).

2. Provided for yourself a place to live without making more mortgage payments, or an equivalent amount of equity.

3. Accumulated enough capital resources (savings) so that (assuming they continue to grow at a modest rate) when you do want to "retire" you can pay yourself what you have decided you need (usually sixty to sixty-five percent of what you are currently spending).

At the close I tell a few stories of how other people have put this idea to work and how doing so has made a difference in their lives and their faith. I get letters or postcards from people telling me they have taken me seriously enough to actually do it.

When this happens, I am on one hand delighted to see the "fruits" of my labor. Preaching is a job in which you receive little evidence of making a difference. So it is a great feeling to hear that people have taken you seriously enough to put what they heard into practice.

On the other hand, I realize how much it can be a mixed blessing to be taken seriously. It scares me silly when this happens. So far, all who have called have told of the great time they are having and thanked me for giving them what they needed to get on with following Christ in all of life. But sooner or later I am bound to get a call from someone who took the plunge and landed headfirst in a empty pool. Or am I?

When God is involved, is there such a thing as an empty pool? Of course not. That is not to say that everyone who takes the plunge into God's second call will have a great experience, or a great time all the time. But it does say that God is good. Following his call leads us into more of his goodness.

The only thing I do with my qualms about what might happen when people take me seriously is to remind both myself and them that God is indeed good. His promise is that we will reside in that goodness as we follow his Son. According to Richard Kiley, the philosopher, "False religion teaches, 'Don't worry, trust God, and nothing bad will happen to you.' True faith says, 'Something bad will probably happen to you, but don't worry, for you can trust God!' "

20

Connecting the Congregation to the Budget

I F I WAS asked to describe one main goal of my stewardship teaching, it would be the necessity of putting God back into the formula. That is to say, being clear that the Sunday morning offering is being given to God in a worship act, rather than to the budget in an economic transaction. This, I believe, is the key to revival in our lives of stewardship. I will continue to insist that congregational stewardship is first and foremost a worship experience.

But at a church in Walnut Creek, Ohio, I came across a situation so dramatically successful that I am adding it to my repertoire of stories for stewardship/ finance committees. I was asked to meet with the people responsible for making up the budgets of this particular congregation. These people call themselves the "board of directors."

When we met I was prepared for the almost universal story of making budgets. That story follows a plot: This year's budget is based on last year's budget plus a 6 percent increase for inflation. Less than a quarter of the congregation shows up at the business meeting to accept it. The budget planners spend the year encouraging (pleading with) the whole congregation to support the budget while commissions underspend their budgets so the cash flow will come out even.

What I heard instead was a story that explained why now there was a waiting list of volunteers to serve on the board and why these directors currently serving are in no hurry to leave! It started when a different group of people with a different attitude about financial management were selected to lead the congregation in stewardship matters. These people (many with a successful business background) told me they changed three things.

1. They prepared what they called a "realistic" budget, one within the realm of possibility of actually being met by the congregation. At the business meeting they presented a preliminary budget tied to what congregational members were giving, rather than what they thought the congregation should give. And then the entire congregation was given the chance to approve or disapprove the new budget when it was presented in a Sunday morning worship service. This changed the attitude of the congregation from one of immediate self-defeat to one of confidence in the goal.

2. They changed the attitude of the treasurer. Rather than having the treasurer charged with "protecting" the money, they focused the job description on making good things happen. Previously any request for additional funds or suggestion of new expenditures was met with a flat "No! there isn't any money!" Now there was a more positive response and often an offer of help with good ideas.

3. They let the congregation know they would include a budget item only if a member of the congregation was personally involved. No longer would money be spent on "detached" good ideas. Now it takes flesh-and-blood involvement to get something added to the list of budget items. Personal involvement means personal commitment. That turns giving into a cheerful joy instead of a dogged chore.

The results of this change were readily visible in this congregation, even if you never got a look at the monthly financial reports or attended the business meetings. During the last session in the series, I went through my list of practical ideas for firstfruits living, such as visiting and working with missionaries the congregation supports and finding work projects instead of vacation sites. I discovered that these people were already doing such things.

Their stewardship leaders had offered them realistic, positive stewardship goals with which they were personally connected. With that sort of encouragement, they had blossomed into a generous and involved group of stewards.

21

Trying Too Hard

A S AN AMATEUR student of church history, especially the Anabaptist portion, I am especially intrigued by how Christians throughout history have attempted to live out Jesus' commandment to "be separate from the world." It seems to me that many of our recent efforts to do so have been in the realm of accommodation.

For example, some groups were once willing to drive cars only if they were black, the sanctioned color. No longer. Anabaptists once rejected insurance, but now most are willing to buy insurance as long as it is sold by an arm of the church. And even the rule forbidding use of the radio in the Hutterite colonies of Manitoba is relaxed for the farm manager who "needs" to know what the weather has in store for the farm.

But recently I have observed two newer attempts to accommodate the values of the world in our circles. One makes me happy, the other amused.

The first example is the recently inaugurated Praxis Mutual Fund offered by Mennonite Mutual Aid, the insurance arm of Mennonite denominations. The creation of this fund drew national attention through its write-up in the *Wall Street Journal*. The attention was deserved because of one feature of the fund. Not only is this a fund with a moral basis for investing—avoiding companies that produce liquor, arms, or tobacco. There is also a provision for tithing profits. An automatic percentage of any profit is to be directed to charitable causes.

This was such an unusual feature of a financial instrument normally designed to increase personal wealth that it stood alone among the thousands of mutual funds. This was something so separate from the world that it drew attention to itself. I am glad to be a part of something different in that way.

The other example amuses me but makes me think we are trying too hard. I was to speak to a group of donors. When I arrived at the dinner site, I was invited to join the assembled guests in a lounge area for hors d'oeuvres. As I stood in line, I was joined by one of the staff who filled me in on the identity of some of the guests and their importance as donors to the continued financial health of the institution. I was impressed that so many people thought well enough of that mission to support it in a major way.

Arriving at the appetizers, I was surprised, however, to be presented with what appeared to be both champagne and caviar. The difference between the denominational identity of this institution and a champagne-and-caviar table was enough to make me take a second look at what was on the table. Then I noticed two things that assured me that even with this leap of hospitality, we were still being true to separation from the world. Instead of champagne, the bottles were full of a nonalcoholic clear sparkling grape juice. And although the caviar was real enough, it was served on plastic plates.

Apparently noticing my reaction, my host asked what I had been thinking. "Do you suppose we are trying too hard?"

I must admit my answer, at least internally, was a resounding "Yes!" I do think we are trying too hard when adopt the gimmicks of the world in fund-raising or anything else. Through such accommodations, we place ourselves in danger of missing the point.

So what is the point? That we can stop trying so hard to be something we are not. We are not really with-it people as the world defines matters. We should just let ourselves be who we are.

Followers of Jesus can still have and treat others with hors d'oeuvres of almost any type, but they need to be *our* hors d'oeuvres, not the world's. We can have mutual funds, but they need to be *our* mutual funds, as MMA's appears to be. It may not look like much from the outside, I suppose, but followers of the living Christ create their own "in-crowd." And following Jesus provides rewards much greater than caviar and champagne.

22

A Contradiction in Terms

E VERY ONCE in a while, I run across what can only be called a contradiction in terms. Otherwise known as an oxymoron, these odd creatures of the English language contain two or more things that are mutually exclusive.

After meeting with businesspeople in eastern Pennsylvania, all of whom belong to the group of Christians called Mennonites, I have discovered a new oxymoron. After I heard their personal stories, I have come to the conclusion that another good oxymoron would be *happy Mennonite businessperson*.

Apparently you can be a happy Mennonite, or a Mennonite businessperson, or even a happy business-person. I am beginning to doubt, however, that you can be all three at once. I suspect this may be true in other varieties of the Christian faith as well.

If we have done well in business, many of us seem to feel vaguely guilty about it, as if doing well is an indication of a wrong motive or a greedy disposition. When putting in long hours trying to get a new business on its feet, you cut back your availability to the church and your own family. Then you get the distinct impression that you are on the verge of committing an almost unforgivable sin.

When you finally succeed in business, you can count on the fund-raisers to show up at your door, seeking their share. Although most Christian businesspeople know the purpose of doing well in business is to do good in the kingdom, it is easy to develop a cynical attitude toward church institutions that at least in part depend on the generosity of businesspeople.

The other side of the coin isn't much prettier. If we do poorly in business, we naturally find it difficult to be happy about it. But we suffer not only from the resulting financial crisis. Many nonbusiness types seem to believe that failure in business is an indication of a deep spiritual problem or even a sign of God's personal disfavor.

Never mind that according to the national average, the majority of business start-ups eventually fail, and half of those in the first two years. We still tend to connect business results and faith. The difference is that now instead of a crowd of fund-raisers knocking on your door, the wolf waiting there has plenty of space. No one wants to be around a business failure.

Frankly, for Christians who claim to take Jesus

more seriously than anything else, I'm surprised at this deplorable state of affairs. Jesus has a lot of positive things to say about the "business of business."

In the parable of the talents in Matthew 25, for example, Jesus says that the one who received the five talents "immediately went and put his money to work." Jesus also describes the employer's response to both the servant's work and the 100 percent profit as a matter of being a "good and faithful servant." On the other hand, the one who hid the money and did not do any business with it was called a "lazy and worthless slave."

In the Luke 19 parallel parable of the ten pounds, the best rate of return was tenfold. Jesus' nobleman tells the slave he is "trustworthy"—hardly an indictment of the slave's business abilities.

In warning about greed and possessions (Luke 12:13-21), Jesus speaks of a rich man whose response to abundant harvest was to build bigger barns. He told himself, "Soul, you have ample goods laid up for many years; relax, eat, drink, and be merry." That very night the rich man died. Jesus says this parable shows what it will be like "with those who store up treasures for themselves but are not rich toward God."

Jesus talks a lot about people doing business. In none of those stories is there any suggestion that the business of doing business is a spiritual problem. But Jesus makes a point: our motive and purpose for doing business make the difference. Our motive is to become "rich toward God." Our purpose is that God's generosity toward us in Christ Jesus be passed on to others in our generosity to them. Maybe it's about time we get down to business, God's business!

23

Love Those Phone Calls

ONE OF the most frustrating kinds of phone calls one normally receives is the fund-raising call that comes right in the middle of dinner. At our house if it isn't the local Benevolent Policeman's Fund or the Great Lakes Division of the National Audubon Society, it will·be the Columbus Symphony Orchestra.

Now we appreciate most of what our local police do to protect the innocent from evil. We like what the Audubon Society does to protect what God has created. We enjoy what the Columbus Symphony Orchestra creates in the way of music.

All of these are good causes. But recently I purchased from the Better Business Bureau a small book that has given me information about how some of these good causes go about doing what they do. Every charitable (nonprofit) organization (except churches and charities with a gross income of less than $25,000) that receives tax-exempt status from the IRS must annually file a form 990. This document includes the most recent financial statement detailing the amount of income received, how it was spent, and what proportion went to actual program services. It also details the salaries of the five highest-paid executives in the organization.

The IRS will send you a copy of any tax-exempt organization's form 990 simply for the asking (and a small copying fee). And in its book the Better Business Bureau lists this information for the 200 most inquired-about charities. It is very interesting information indeed.

For example, I was surprised to find that in 1993 the highest-paid executive in the American Red Cross wasn't their national CEO but the director of the southern California region, whose compensation exceeded $340,000. And although the National Audubon Society's CEO receives only $178,000 per year, in 1993 they were also only able to deliver 58 percent of their income to program services. And neither the Christian Broadcasting Network nor Concerned Women of America will tell the Better Business Bureau anything about their finances.

None of this says that these are not reputable charities doing good works. But since we want our generosity to do as much good work as possible, my spouse and I will be making a few changes in our charitable giving, now that we have this information.

The best thing that has happened, however, is that we now love receiving those annoying phone calls. Even at the dinner table. For now we have two things at the table along with dinner. First, we have the Better

Business Bureau's little book. Second, for those charities not in the book, we have a large-print copy of the following response taped to the cover of the book.

> Thank you very much for calling us. If you will send us your latest financial statement, and a description of your organization's work, we will be glad to consider your request.

By responding to fund-raising phone calls this way, we've discovered several things. First, fundraisers for honest charities are glad to honor your request for information. They know that the more you know about them, the larger your financial involvement in their future will likely be. Second, the telemarketing people who were selling aluminum replacement windows yesterday and raising money for a charity today usually say "Thank you," then hang up. They know that spending time with you will not help them raise their personal receipts and commissions.

The funny part is that I am almost always sad when they do hang up, for I love being generous with the abundance God has given me.

24

Crippled by the
Little Things

I N 1994 Linda and I were invited to participate in the
Heritage Wooden Boat Festival held at the Chicago
Corinthian Yacht Club. We were invited because four
years earlier I had built a seventeen-foot classic wood-
en sailboat designed by a rather famous naval architect
named L. Francis Herreshoff, a design recognized and
appreciated by classic boat lovers everywhere.

We had a great time sailing and displaying our boat
along the shores of Lake Michigan. We had such a
good time partly because in the twelve-mile race
twenty-three boats entered on Friday, we came in
seventh, even though we had the shortest waterline
length and therefore were expected to be the slowest
boat.

But something happened late Saturday evening

that left me rather crippled by Monday morning. While I was cleaning up around our mooring at the end of the wooden dinghy dock, I tried to move a small piece of equipment on the dock with my foot. I ended up with a splinter of dock wood in my left big toe.

Less than forty-eight hours later, my whole left foot looked like a football. Although I couldn't actually see the flames, I was sure the end of my big toe was on fire! I had been incapacitated by a piece of wood smaller than one-fourth of a toothpick.

Once in awhile in my travels, I meet someone likewise crippled in their lives of stewardship by equally small events. For example, I recently met a man who told me he gives most of his money to organizations outside of his home church. Ten years ago he disagreed with other members over how much housing allowance should be designated for the pastor, even though that allocation between cash salary and housing did not cost the church anything extra.

Another person told me that once he saw the hotels the denominational executives stayed at during a church conference, he decided they had too much money to spend on accommodations. He reduced his giving to those agencies accordingly.

There is no doubt that both of these individuals were hurt by what they had experienced in their past. Considering the scope of their lives of stewardship, it is also clear that both of these "slights" were minor. But it is equally true that they both are currently crippled by those experiences. Perhaps, my skeptical ear wonders, they are just using those excuses to be less generous than they could be. Either way, they have

taken their "splinters" so seriously that they a
truly incapacitated by them.

Perhaps that is the clue for pulling out these kinds
of splinters. The solution is to take them less seriously.
If we put them into perspective, if we reduce their importance in our own worldview, then we would be less
crippled by them. In my experience as a pastor, I was
more than once impressed by our ability to choose not
to be offended by actions of others.

Several people at that boat festival wanted me to
see a doctor about the splinter in my toe. I replied that
I might do just that later if my body did not expel the
foreign object in its own way by festering and swelling.
But I refused to let that little splinter affect how I
would respond to future invitations to be part of something that is so much fun. Likewise, I am committed
not to let the little irritations of life dictate how I live.
Or give!

25

They Just Don't Get It

MOST PEOPLE have heard about the common male experience of midlife crisis. This refers to a period in many men's lives, usually between ages thirty-five and forty-five, when they no longer are satisfied merely to be either well-paid or good at what they do. Now their careers and their lives are measured in terms of meaning. When meaning is lacking, the primary emotion is an overwhelming feeling of hopelessness.

The most effective solution to getting through this difficult time of life is not buying a red sports car or finding a younger wife. The answer is to find real significance in what one does. I know this because in the spring of 1988 I went through my own midlife crisis, and emerged thankful that I would never have to experience that again.

However, in the middle of the final worship service of a national church conference I attended, I got that same hopeless feeling all over again. For over five years I had been preaching about the worship offering as a pure gift to God in thankfulness for what we have already received. It should therefore be an exciting and major part of the service. But now, after listening to the worship leader go on and on about receiving an offering for several worthy projects, then being forced to sit quietly in my seat while little plastic yogurt cups were passed in the silent congregation, I heard myself say, *They just didn't get it!*

In the first service the worship leader said we were taking an offering to cover $40,000 in conference expenses. Nothing was said about our motivation for giving, about thankfulness for the death and resurrection of Jesus Christ, about the indwelling and gifts of the Holy Spirit, about God.

A number of people came up to me after each worship service and commented on the difference between what I had been teaching and what we had just done. Apparently the worship planning committee was made up of the last six people in that denomination who hadn't heard about taking offerings in a way that makes them exciting gifts to an extravagant God. That was a depressing thought: they just hadn't gotten it.

Then I remembered what happened at the Christian Workers Conference I spoke at in Boise, Idaho. Several hundred believers had gathered there to do work projects, learn from God's Word, and offer praise in our combined meetings at the YWCA. After five sessions, and a wonderful final worship service that Sunday morning, the conference leader told the gathering that we had done everything we were planning to do. Since we had a few minutes left, she asked if there was anything they wanted to do. Another hymn? Another chorus? Any last thing before she closed the conference with prayer?

After a moment of silence, a woman's voice came from the back of the room. "Can we take another offering?" We had already taken two offerings in a variety of exciting ways. The expenses of the conference had already been met and exceeded.

So the moderator replied, "No, we have enough money."

There was a slight pause. Then back came the right answer, "We aren't taking it for you!"

When the applause and laughter died down, we found cardboard boxes to hold our contributions since the offering baskets had already been returned to the church. We celebrated as we gave a third offering, not for expenses, not for conference, not even for missions, just for God! There was more in that last offering than in the first two combined!

I need to remember that Sunday in Boise when I get the feeling that someone else just doesn't get it. Those people at Boise got it!

26

Firstfruits Family Evangelism

S OMETIMES we can learn a lot about effective evangelism just by listening to the story of someone else's faith journey. A man I had never met called and invited me to have breakfast with him to talk about our mutual interest in church history. But first we told our own stories to each other. Right in the middle of his story, I heard a description of what can only be called "firstfruits family evangelism."

This fellow and his wife had just moved to a new area of the country. Like many new residents, they had put off looking for a new church home while they made other arrangements in their recently disrupted life. Before they had a chance to experience any of the various Sunday morning church-growth techniques currently in place in the surrounding congregations (with full color brochures, rotating noon-meal hosts), they were "captured" by the simplest technique of all. The neighbor next door came to visit and quickly discovered that these new neighbors were from several states away. Now they wouldn't be able to visit the family home as much as they had previously. So the neighbor insisted they celebrate the coming Thanksgiving with his family.

Not much later, when they had gotten to know each other much better and had established some common ground, that neighbor invited the couple to a few social and recreational events he and his circle of friends attended. A few months later, he invited them to join those same friends for their Sunday school class at the local United Methodist Church.

Now that's pretty simple. Establish a friendship. Widen the circle of friendships. Finally include the Sabbath in the activities. Nothing revolutionary there. But this story is different. For these relocated folks were Mennonites. Although they had moved to an area in which there were half a dozen Mennonite congregations nearby, this couple was "captured" by a congregation with a different history and traditions.

"So, what was so attractive about the United Methodists?" I asked him.

"Not a thing," he replied. "In fact, I miss the simplicity of a Mennonite worship service."

"Was it something that particular congregation did to make you feel welcome the first time you attended?" I pressed, hoping to hear of a new and irresistible "narthex gimmick."

"No. There wasn't anything special about the congregation at all. But by the time we actually attended for the first time, it was like going to church with our own extended family. When we showed up at the front door of the church, we were surrounded by a whole new set of brothers and sisters and aunts and uncles and cousins. There is nothing quite as comfortable as going to church with people you know well enough to call 'family.' "

Most of us know a lot about family. All you have to do to see them is just to look around the sanctuary about ten minutes after the service is over. There they are, in little groups checking in about the next week's activities and last week's results. The problem is that to become part of most of those families, you have to marry one of their members. Most families are closed small groups, open only to relatives.

Maybe opening those closed groups will take seeing our family relationships as another kind of offering, an "offering" to new neighbors. Instead of saving the firstfruits of relationships for ourselves—the Thanksgiving and Christmas family gatherings—we could offer them to those who need them the most.

Maybe becoming a "firstfruit to the rest of God's creatures" (Jas. 1:18) will mean opening family circles to help our families grow so our congregations can grow. Then the church can truly become *God's family* in each locality, a place where others can feel they belong (Mark 3:34-35; Rom. 8:14-17, 29). After all, as my new friend said, there is nothing quite as comforting as going to church with your family.

27

It Really Works

ONE OF the embarrassing things that happens when you think that taking Jesus seriously means actually trying to love your enemies and returning good for evil is that sooner or later someone is going to say, "Yeah, but what would you do if—?" Then they offer a scary "kill or be killed" scenario in which the only choices presented are being violent or the victim of violence. Blessedly, most people can answer that challenge without being burdened with thinking through a past experience.

But just before Christmas 1995, Linda and I had the chance to live through what till then was only a hypothetical situation. At 8:00 in the morning, in broad daylight, we were held up at gunpoint as we were walking to church. We had been warned that this might happen in our neighborhood of Chicago, and I had practiced a number of ways to respond nonviolently. Like, "Neat gun! What kind is it? What caliber?" Or, "You don't know this, but at this moment I'm wearing boxer shorts and I'm prepared to use them!"

We were hurrying to the parsonage to give our condolences to the pastor's wife, who had called to tell us her mother had died that morning. We cut across an empty lot behind the liquor store, across Van Buren Street, then down the short alley that leads to her back door. Halfway there I spotted a roofing nail lying in the alley, just waiting to give someone a flat tire. I stopped, bent over, picked up the nail, and straightened up to find myself looking at a person standing right in front of me.

I showed him the nail and told him I had just saved someone five dollars.

But his response was, "Give me your money!" And that's when I noticed the ski mask, and the gun.

I never thought of even one of my clever answers to the hypothetical "What if?" I told him I had no money, but if he would come with us to church, we would try to find something for him. He waved the gun and shouted again for me to give the money. I repeated that I didn't have any but we could find something for him at church.

Then Linda told him we needed to visit a woman whose mother had just died. We both turned and started to walk down the narrow path to the back of the church. Halfway there, when I had stopped wondering what getting shot in the back was going to feel like, I turned around and said, "Come on." I motioned for him to follow. He just stood there, then turned and ran.

Most people here have since told us that we were

either lucky or crazy. They have advised that we should carry a roll of bills just for such an occasion, to be a "better victim." Others have offered various ways of defending ourselves. I don't know for sure why he didn't shoot us right then and there. After all, it happens at least twice a day somewhere in Chicago.

However, I'm beginning to think that giving the assailant an invitation that had his needs in mind was what made it work. Maybe the combination of offering something that would help him achieve what he wanted without showing disrespect for the power of his gun, kept him from pulling the trigger.

Despite the fact that when it happened, I couldn't think of anything I had practiced, I'm now preparing something different. Instead of responses that are self-protecting and nonviolent, now I rehearse responses that seek good for my assailant. For nonviolent self-defense is still self-defense. And the work of Jesus is to find good for the other. After all, in the midst of our crime (sin), Jesus Christ found good for us.

28

Self-Interest and Morality

O CCASIONALLY in one of my stewardship seminars, I am asked to define what the legal parameters are for an IRS-approved charitable deduction. As I understand the letter and spirit of the U.S. tax code, the definition hinges on what we call "self-interest." To legally claim a gift to a church as a charitable deduction, we must let go of our "self-interest."

For example, although we can give a cash donation to a general fund or building fund and claim the gift as a charitable deduction, we cannot require or direct that our gift be used only for a specific expenditure. Likewise, although we can make a gift to a student-aid fund (one in which proceeds of the fund are divided equally among qualified students), we cannot claim a deduction for a gift made to such a fund if our *expectation* is that our own child will receive that same amount. We must separate ourselves from our self-interest for our gifts to be tax deductible.

Interestingly enough, this same principle of denying self-interest also underlies the teaching of Jesus concerning gifts. In Matthew 6:1-5 Jesus warns us about our motivations for giving. "But when you give alms, do not let your left hand know what your right hand is doing." This refers to the practice of giving one thing only so another thing is received, in this case the reward of honor and esteem from others. The hypocrites, Jesus says, do their giving "in the streets and synagogues after sounding a trumpet, just so they may be honored by men." In following verses Jesus says the hypocrites pray "in the synagogues and on the street corners in order to be seen by men."

Unfortunately, much of the modern Christian church (at least in the U.S.) seems to have a lower standard of morality than not only Jesus but also of the IRS. In 1994 the IRS began requiring that any charitable gift over $250 be proved by a receipt from the recipient. This new requirement came about because the IRS discovered that many Christians were making tuition payments to church-owned schools their children attended and claiming them to be charitable deductions simply because they gave them through the Sunday morning offering.

Not allowed, says the IRS. Like Jesus, the IRS demands that we give up our self-interest. No wonder the government is suspicious of "religious" influence in the affairs of a nation. Too many of us haven't done a good job of giving them something to cheer about.

I know one man, however, who because of his "outrageous generosity," is regularly given a chance to witness to the government about God's generosity at the cross. This fellow and his wife consistently give away over 40 percent of their income. Every two or three years they are called into the IRS regional office for an audit.

When I asked if he was getting irritated at being continually audited, he replied, "Not at all. Think about it," he continued, "if I called the IRS up and asked for an appointment to tell one of their agents in their office on their time about the outrageous generosity of the cross, they would just laugh at me and hang up. But if I give more than 40 percent of my income away, every so often they insist that I come to their offices to tell them why. That forces me to tell them exactly the same thing!"

Maybe this is how the church can undo the damage done to the witness of Christ by Christians caught cheating on their income taxes. Maybe more of us should give so generously that we get audited. And when they ask why, we can tell them it's a response of thanksgiving to God for what we have already received. Now that is an IRS audit to look forward to!

As the apostle Peter says, "Sanctify Christ as Lord in your hearts, always being ready to make a defense to every one who asks you to give an account for the hope that is in you, yet with gentleness and reverence" (1 Pet. 3:15). So what if the IRS calls us "to give an account"? Think of it, a whole new witnessing technique—"audit-evangelism"!

29

Disposer of Human Remains

ONE OF the more important events for me in 1995 was the death of my father, Eugene D. Miller. Most significantly, although I was still traveling full-time and at the same time living in Ohio, I was able to be with him at his home in Santa Cruz, California, during his last week of life and his last hours. A blessed but difficult gift.

Two weeks after his death, his family and friends gathered together in the redwoods of the California coast to remember this man. He had had several successful careers, built a number of houses, sailboats, and experimental aircraft. In his retirement years he was a neighbor and good friend to many in the coastal mountains overlooking Monterey Bay. Mom's brother played his guitar and sang the old gospel song "Angel

Band." I led the assembled group in the telling of "Gene" stories. We scattered about half of his ashes in a flower bed on a large old redwood stump.

Then my brother and sister and I planted a young Granny Smith apple tree in his memory. We placed the rest of the ashes around the root ball as we filled in the hole. Finally I led the group in a short prayer to end the service.

Later that afternoon, I signed the "Application and Permit for the Disposition of Human Remains" to indicate to the authorities of California that what had remained of Eugene David Miller had been disposed of properly. Except, as I quickly discovered when I turned the paper over, I was wrong! Oh, the remains were certainly disposed of. They were scattered in two different places on the grounds of the Fern Flat Fine Fruit Farm. But they had not been *properly* disposed of. On the reverse side of the permit, in large capital letters, was printed the following special instruction:

CREMATED REMAINS SHALL NOT BE SCATTERED OVER INLAND WATERS OR OVER LAND UNLESS IN A DEDICATED CEMETERY IN A GARDEN AREA USED EXCLUSIVELY FOR SUCH PURPOSES.

Oops! One rule my father lived by was always to read the instructions first! By not doing so, I had broken the California State Health and Safety Code, Sections 7054.6, 7054.7, 7117, 10376, and 10376.5. The site at which his ashes were scattered was in no way a "dedicated cemetery in a garden area used exclusively for such purposes." Too late now. I'll just have to pay the penalty for my misdeed whenever the state of California informs me what it is.

In the meantime I am left with a new designation in my pastoral bag-of-tricks—"disposer of human remains." I rather like that designation, for recently I have again disposed of human remains. But this time my own "remains." Not my ashes, for despite the burned-out feeling I have occasionally, I am still kicking. What I disposed of were my other remains, those things that remain after we are gone, what we call an "estate." I finally did what I had been planning for some time. I established our family's "charitable gift fund," complete with instructions for how our eventual "remains" are to be disposed of.

The whole process was simple and didn't require an application or permit. It took only three steps: (1) signing a form establishing a charitable gift fund in our name with our denomination's charitable foundation, (2) naming the foundation as a beneficiary in our wills and in our gift fund, and (3) naming which missions and charitable institutions we wish our "remains" to be distributed among and in what proportions. That was it!

Now all I have to do is hope and pray that the foundation reads and follows my recommendations more carefully than I observed California's rules!

30

Remember Who
You Are

S HORTLY AFTER starting my first pastorate, I sensed
the "cultural distinctives" of that particular community. Every faith community has its own distinctives, but these were the first of this variety I had come
across, so I remember them well. Especially the phrase
thrown at the backs of youth of the church as they left
their parents' watchful gaze and began moving about
in the broader community. Again and again I heard
stories of young people being told, "Remember who
you are," as they went out the door.

I never could tell if the parents' intent was to encourage them to keep in mind their community con-
nections and its moral standards, or to warn them that
if they shamed that community, they would pay. Either
way, "Remember who you are" isn't a bad thing to say

to a church as its members go into the world to be exhibits of God's grace.

Of all the churches I have seen over the years, there are two kinds I remember. The first type are those I would be willing to move near so I could attend there, then go looking for a job. These are exciting churches, full of vigor and vision, with people who are enthusiastic about being "church." They sit close together, in a big clump in the middle of the sanctuary, and forward, even in the front rows!

On the other hand, if I had the authority, I would close some churches. Their congregational life brings shame on the name of Jesus Christ. These are congregations at war with each other, where people come only to keep other people from getting away with anything. They don't trust each other, their leadership, or anything from denominational sources.

The only difference between these two kinds of congregations, as far as I can tell, is this: the former know and remember who they are. The latter don't want to be what little they know of themselves.

The exciting congregations are full of people who know who they are, both theologically and historically. They know the stories of how their foreparents lived out the gospel of Jesus Christ. They know the price their ancestors paid for their faith. These people are not ashamed of their cultural or theological identity. They love the rituals of their church, including the "holy potluck" (the fourth sacrament right behind baptism, communion, and footwashing). They love those rituals because by doing them regularly, they remind themselves of who they are.

Other congregations neither grow nor glow. They resist association with any particular history. They include a vocal minority anxious to replace a denominational name with "Community." They take an anti-institutional stance whenever and wherever possible. Being against the right things, opposing other people's sins, and making sure the boundaries are clearly drawn and aggressively defended—this will draw the loyalty of like-minded crusaders. But these congregations will not bring in neighbors, friends, or relatives. After all, if you don't like what's going on, why would you invite anyone else to come? Who would want to join a group that is at war with itself?

But if you're an enthusiast for the way of Jesus as understood by those who have gone before you, then you're not threatened by new people or their diversity. If you know who you are, you can invite people to learn about that identity *and* to join you in a common expression of loyalty to Jesus from that perspective. If you like being who you are, a result of knowing just what it is that there is to remember, then you know what it is that unites your particular congregation.

That produces fun, because then you can trust the people who sit next to you. You can trust the people who stand before you. If you know who you are, you can be who you are, and get on with it!

The world is full of people who want to be somebody. Many are finding that identity in a clothing brand or automobile model. But nothing is more attractive than a group of people who are both at peace and excited about who they are, who are then free to focus on the One they follow.

31

In the Right Place at the Right Time!

O NE OF the most important church-planting questions is, What is the right place for the new
church? Usually the right answer has to do with population demographics or land prices. But after visiting
Matamoros, Mexico, where a church called Templo
Menonita Nueva Jerusalem was planted, I now know
what it means to be in the "right place at the right
time."

The New Jerusalem Mennonite Church is a small
congregation doing the right thing in the right place at
the right time. Their simple two-story concrete block
building is in the middle of the biggest red-light dis-
trict in town. Church is held downstairs, and the
pastor's family lives upstairs. On our drive through the
narrow streets of Matamoros to the church, we saw in-

creasingly deteriorating neighborhoods. As we approached the church itself, we saw that degeneration in human lives. Even at 7:00 p.m. there were drunks outside the bars and prostitutes on every corner.

With the passage of the North American Free Trade Act (NAFTA), and the rapid expansion of export manufacturing, U.S. businesses are building factories south of the border as fast as they can. Each day more people are leaving their rural villages in the south of Mexico and coming to the border, looking for work.

On a visit to a *maquiladora* (a U.S. factory in Mexico), we saw several hundred young men and women working ten-hours shifts, gluing handles to J. C. Penney paper shopping bags. These workers received twenty pesos a day three pesos more than the Mexican minimum wage. Before devaluation that was equivalent to $5.70 (U.S.) but now equaled only $3.70. *Three dollars and seventy cents a day!* Even at that rate, there are plenty of applicants, many more than jobs. Yet still they come, flooding the border areas with a sea of unemployed humanity, looking for a better life, a brighter future.

What does this have to do with Templo Menonita Nueva Jerusalem in Matamoros being in the right place at the right time? Just this. Some of the women who came north with their husbands and families, looking for honest work, have been forced into prostitution to keep themselves and their children alive. Their husbands have swum the Rio Grande and, if not caught by the Border Patrol, they are seeking work as "illegals" in Brownsville, Texas, and on the farms along the northern side of the river. But the women are left with the children in Matamoros, and the children are left to fend for themselves while the mothers are on the street corners.

That is why Templo Menonita de la Nueva Jerusalem is in the right place at the right time. Pastor Rafael Garcia and his flock have a children's program on the church grounds, a program specifically designed to minister to the physical and spiritual needs of the children of the prostitutes.

Think about that for a moment. Would they be able to do that if the church were located in a nice clean suburb? Would they be able to offer the grace of God to those people located on the other side of the border? If this was something they were thinking about doing someday, sometime, would it make these children's lives better today, now? Of course not.

It strikes me that this is also a matter of firstfruits stewardship. These Christians have decided that their first priority is to be a church that is an offering to those who need them the most. They could have a larger church somewhere else. But they are doing the right thing, God's thing, in the right place, God's place, at the right time, God's time! Hallelujah! *Gloria a Dios!*

32

Not Just Showing Up

W HEN I AM leading a seminar at a congregation, one of the unexpected roles I often play is that of sounding board for the "pastorally dissatisfied." Sometime during my visit, usually during a meal in a member's home, I am asked what I would do about a situation in a hypothetical congregation where many of the members are dissatisfied with the pastor's work among them—usually the preaching. When I ask, "So what exactly is it that you don't like about the preaching?" most hosts begin to list the points.

But this usually only happens before the session in which I describe what a firstfruits gift of worship looks like, and before I have told of the family who visited our home and complained about their home church. When they said they were contemplating a move to another church because they weren't getting everything they wanted at their present church, I replied that I agreed that they should indeed change.

However, I said, they should not go to another church. Instead, they should go to the mall on Sunday mornings. The mall is where you go to "get everything you want." Church is where you come to bring everything God wants—worship!

I have found another way to approach the point. There is a story about an English professor at Columbia University, Raymond Weaver. At the end of a semester, he began a quiz by writing on the chalkboard, "Which of the required readings in this course did you find least interesting?" As his students happily divulged their dissatisfactions with the readings, he wrote the second question: "To what defect in yourself do you attribute this lack of interest?"

Imagine a congregational survey with the following two questions:

1. What portion of the worship service do you find least satisfying?

2. To what defect in your spiritual condition do you attribute this dissatisfaction?

If I could effect one change in attitudes of the people I speak to, it would be in why people go to church. I would like to convince them that worship is not a matter of just showing up. The intent in our hearts pleases God, not our mere presence in the pews or our money.

Then, because renewal of ourselves is at the root of the gospel, I would add a third question:

3. What changes in yourself do you want to make to increase God's satisfaction with our worship?

Putting God's satisfaction before ours is a good first step to firstfruits living.

33

What Kind of
Church Is This?

M OST OF us at one time or another have observed
some sort of minor distraction in the midst of a
Sunday school class or a worship service. You know
what I mean—babies crying, children talking, the occasional snoring adult. If we aren't amused by the distraction, at least we're tolerant. But for the person
teaching the class or leading the service, those moments can be particularly annoying.

Annoyance was the feeling I had during a Sunday
seminar I was leading in a small inner-city Ohio
church. During Sunday school, I had to compete with a
stream of people coming and going in a futile effort to
make the sound system work. Then right in the middle
of the lesson, we were interrupted. First it was a man
who had come in off the street demanding to see one

of the young women in the class. Next it was a horde of delinquent children who had escaped their own classes.

Sadly, the worship service wasn't much better. During the message at least half of the two dozen adults present left the room at least twice.

During the carry-in dinner following the service, a "bag lady" came in from the street asking for food. Even from a distance, we could see she had both nostrils stuffed with cloth. When I passed her, it took only one whiff to discover why. Even she couldn't stand the smell that surrounded her.

In the session that followed lunch, the sound system began making terminally obscene noises every minute or so. What a crazy place! The only thing I could think was, "What kind of church is this?"

I already knew this congregation had been started by a larger suburban congregation as a "clone." They had made a conscious decision to divide rather than build. They wanted to plant the new congregation in the poorest area of the city, where they believed they could be of service to the community. They bought an old brick church building that was empty, and the large number of families committed to being the core of this new congregation began attending.

But over the past number of years, as the work of building an interracial congregation proved more difficult than expected, most of the members who had left the mother church to plant the new congregation returned to the familiar safety of the suburban church. On this particular day, some sixteen years later, I was speaking to the "remnant"—one original family and the four or five local families who had joined since.

My last session was on how a congregation becomes an offering to the world that surrounds it. During the following discussion, I commented that all day I had been having trouble deciding what kind of congregation this was.

They replied, "That's what we're trying to figure out!" For the next thirty minutes, we worked on just what kind of church God wanted them to be.

We discovered that for the past sixteen years these people had been trying to be something God had not called them to be. They had tried to be a "traditional" church. They were trying to be a clone of the suburban congregation, ministering to the suburban families that drove in to attend Sunday services, yet reaching out by inviting neighborhood families to join them. But they in fact had become much more of a "service center" for the poor and dispossessed in the neighborhood that surrounded them.

That was what all the distractions were about. People were coming to be ministered to, Sunday morning or not! From the end of Sunday school through the first half of worship, people were mediating the conflict with the young man who had interrupted the class. Others had withdrawn to offer intercessory prayer. People came and went during the service to care for the large contingent of foster and adopted children in the congregation. The sound system was lousy because these few people had better things to do with their money, like feeding bad-smelling bag ladies.

I was wasting my time teaching these folks how to be God's offering to the world. Without knowing it, that was exactly what they had been doing all along.

34

That'll Preach!

S OMETIMES the hardest part of sermon preparation is finding just the right illustration to make the connection between the biblical text and a person's life. Sometimes if you keep your eyes open and follow the Spirit's leading, God will give you the illustration you need. When you see it, you know it: "That'll preach!"

I was once asked to be resource speaker to two different groups of 250 or so teenagers at a snow camp in northern Pennsylvania. The topic was "Alien Nation: The Christian's Place in the World." I had diligently prepared for the three sessions I was responsible for. But when I arrived I still hadn't found the perfect illustration for the Christian life. God blessed us by using those teenagers to give me the illustration.

While I was walking that afternoon and trying to think of the perfect illustration, I noticed a group of young people heading the same direction through the woods. I followed them to what looked like a shallow but well-sculptured water diversion ditch that came swooping down a steep hill and ended in a sweeping curve at the bottom of the slope. The purpose of this landscape became plain a few moments later when five screaming teenagers lying on an inflated tractor-tire inner tube went flying past. This was Camp Hebron's famous snow-slick "Tubing Run."

Watching was fun. But when a group that went flying past invited me to walk with them back to the top of the run, I couldn't resist. At the top I just stood there on my shaking half-century-old legs and watched these exuberant teenagers try every variation of getting as many as possible otherwise sane human beings down the hill as fast as they could.

Then it happened. One group of four invited me to join them on their run. When I agreed, two girls immediately flopped face-down on a small tube and two guys piled on behind them. I sat upright on a second tube, and a final person sat in my lap facing forward and holding the legs of the guys in front of me.

Off we went. It was fun, it really was. We went flying down the chute, over what felt like a couple of small hills, and leaned into the curve at the bottom. From my position as the hindmost person, I couldn't see well, but it looked like a reasonably safe journey. So I followed that same group back up the hill.

At the top they included me in the plans for their next descent. But this time they insisted that we use one of the big-tractor-size tubes. They decided that I should be on the bottom and up front since I was the heaviest and thus would provide the most inertia (a good example of being abused by education.)

So I was placed on the bottom in the middle, with my head sticking a foot out in front of the tube. Two kids piled on next to me but a little bit further back on the tube. Two more piled on top of the three of us.

Off we went. But this time I suddenly realized two important things. First, this toboggan run was a lot steeper and more dangerous than I had thought. The first time down, I hadn't seen the ski jump that immediately preceded the cliff in the middle of the course. And although I had seen them earlier, I hadn't realized how close the trees were to the course and how hard they looked. With my head in front of everything else, I would be the first personally to experience that fact.

My second insight was that there was nothing I could do to address my first insight. With four people on top of me, I couldn't get off. With my feet and hands smothered under 500 pounds of humans, I couldn't even stick anything out to slow down. And it quickly became apparent that no matter who leaned which way, the thing was unsteerable. There was nothing I could do. I could only relax and enjoy the ride.

I did! It was great! Halfway between the ski jump and the cliff, I realized we didn't need to steer. The course had been designed to allow the tubes to slide sideways toward the trees only so far before gravity pulled them into the center of the chute again. Praise God for gravity! When we reached the flatter part of the run, we shot past where most of the smaller groups had slid to a stop. Praise God for inertia! And when we got to the bottom, the only thing I could say was, "That'll preach, that'll preach!"

You see, that is what joining God's kingdom is like. First, it comes by invitation. As I was chosen by that group to join them, so God chooses us. Peter writes to those who reside as "aliens . . . chosen by the foreknowledge of God. . . ." That chosenness comes not by consideration of what our qualifications are. Being chosen by God comes from the character of the chooser. Placing me in the front at the bottom came out of considering where my gifts could best be used. But the original invitation to be part of that tubing run came from the hospitality of the group, not from their assessment of what I could do for them.

Second, God's plans for our life with him come apart from our control. The first step to a life of following Jesus is surrender, not victory. Only when we give up control is there room for God's control, for God's engineering to take effect and determine both our safety and our effectiveness.

Finally, just as a group of five can go much farther down the course than one, following Jesus is a group activity. The church is not just one person here and one there trusting Jesus for their eternal destination. The church is the people of God together doing the work of Jesus, work that cannot be done well or sometimes even at all by isolated individuals.

Did it preach? I gave the illustration that evening. Following worship next morning, the camp staff had to open the otherwise closed tubing run because there were so many kids who wanted to experience the illustration before they left for home.

On my way home, I thought how clever God was to have created snow, gravity, and inertia!

The Author

L YNN MILLER is author of *Firstfruits Living* (Herald Press, 1991) and has recently completed a three-and-a-half year (Mennonite) Churchwide Stewardship Council assignment as traveling stewardship teacher. He has visited over 250 churches with the message of firstfruits stewardship.

A Mennonite by choice, Lynn has a B.S. in agriculture and an M.Div. from Goshen (Ind.) Biblical Seminary. He has had experience in farming, rural development with Mennonite Central Committee in southern Africa, and as pastor of the South Union Mennonite Church in West Liberty, Ohio.

Lynn and his wife, Linda, are now in Mennonite Voluntary Service and live in the East Garfield Park neighborhood of Chicago, where they work, respectively, in housing repair and community health. They are parents of two adult daughters, Lori and Lianna.